I

KNOW JUST

HOW YOU

FEEL

...avoiding the cliches of grief

by

ERIN LINN

I KNOW JUST HOW YOU FEEL

...avoiding the cliches of grief

by

ERIN LINN

Illustrated by Art Peterson

The Publisher's Mark
P.O. Box 6939
Incline Village, Nevada 89450

Copyright © 1986
Library of Congress Catalog Card Number: 85-90509
ISBN: 0-9614636-1-9

Printed in the United States of America

ACKNOWLEDGMENTS

While I have had strong support from so many, there are special people who have helped me create I Know Just How You Feel... avoiding the cliches of grief.

Pat Mesch, who has been my mentor, and more importantly, my friend during the course of this work.

Jan Kunzman Bailey, who guided me in the early stages of my book through friendship and encouragement.

Claire Lee Erickson and Maryan Schotanus, friends who spent countless hours editing my book.

Susan Fadem, who helped mold this book into form.

Chris, a wonderful son and inspiration for my work.

Herman, who has given me a steady rock to lean against as only a loving husband can.

ABOUT THE AUTHOR

Erin Linn was born and raised in Port Arthur, Texas. She graduated from the University of Texas and taught school in her native state. Her first book, *Children Are Not Paper Dolls . . . a visit with bereaved siblings,* was written as a result of the death of her son, Michael, combined with a growing concern for the bereavement of children. Ms. Linn's second book, *I Know Just How You Feel . . avoiding the cliches of grief,* tackles the topic of what to say to a bereaved person. The book does this with great energy, insight, compassion, and even a dash of humor. In 1978 she became actively involved in The Compassionate Friends, a national organization for bereaved parents. Since then she has worked with schools, churches, and hospitals, and has been a participant in numerous conferences, workshops, and seminars on death and mourning. Ms. Linn has appeared on talk shows throughout the country and is a frequent guest speaker. Her newest book, *150 Facts About Grieving Children,* is a reflection of her continuing interest and involvement with the bereaved. Ms. Linn now resides in Incline Village, Nevada, with her husband.

DEDICATION

This book is dedicated to all who have shared their pain with me in the hope that a new level of love and understanding can exist between the comforter and the comforted. They are the heart of this book.

INTRODUCTION

Throughout our lives, most of us spend some time being comforted or being the comforter, being consoled or being the consoler. Both roles are painfully difficult and, at times, can be overwhelming. I have been in both roles. In 1974 my six-year old son, Michael, was hit by a car and died instantly. Before this tragic incident I had no idea it was possible to hurt with such intensity. When others would speak of their losses I really thought I understood. I said things like, "That's too bad," or "Time will heal." Then I would retreat into my own little world of security. I did hurt for these people, but it was so hard to relate to a level of pain that I, myself, had never experienced. It wasn't until my own son died that I realized the truth. I did not know what it was like to receive the third strike, and furthermore, I wasn't even in the same emotional ballpark with the bereaved person. This book is an attempt to bridge this gap for others.

Through years of work with bereaved people and of hearing the desperate plight of those who want to comfort the bereaved, I am convinced that the misunderstandings that exist between the two can be avoided. This is a unique opportunity for the comforter and the comforted to listen to each other. It is my hope that through these pages the comforter will find new ways to approach the bereaved through love that is sensitive and productive. It is also my wish that the bereaved will find comfort in this book by seeing that what may appear as insensitive comments from relatives and friends are really words of love. Sometimes they are simply expressed in a clumsy, awkward way. As a bereaved person, try to keep in mind that the comforter is, also, searching for answers and ways to deal with these tragedies.

We must draw from the goodness that is in each of us as a place to begin. It is human nature to want to reach out and help those who are in pain. When we know of someone who is grieving, we go to them with words and actions that we hope will both soothe and comfort. Unfortunately, our soothing words may be the most feared of all verbal weapons - the cliche. By its very definition, a cliche - a trite and commonplace expression - is misused and overworked. There is a desperate need for the comforter to supply an answer or provide a remedy for the bereaved person's pain lest they fail to really help. As a result, with cliches we attempt to provide simple solutions to overwhelming situations. We use stale phrases to nourish the bereaved, just as we use T.V. dinners to feed a computerized society.

If we speak from our hearts with all the honesty and love we each possess, these canned remedies - cliches -

will not be necessary. Besides, there is no answer that truly explains a tragedy such as death in a way that our human faculties can comprehend. We should not feel compelled to produce an explanation no matter how much we care. Trite sayings fall short of expressing our real feelings, and can offend the person to whom they are said even though our intentions are honorable. (Comments that cause pain often stay with the newly bereaved longer and can become more intense as time passes.)

How to approach the bereaved person is something that people have agonized over since the beginning of time. How often have we said or heard someone say, "What can I say to them?" How often has the bereaved person asked, "Why did they say that to me?" This book will begin to answer these questions that have existed for far too long. There is an uncomfortable, helpless feeling no matter which side of the fence you are on. So if you see yourself in these pages don't worry. It proves you are human - what a wonderful way to be.

CONTENTS

"BE STRONG" CLICHES
Big boys don't cry.   16
The children are flexible ...   18
    they will bounce back.
You must be strong for your children.   21
Support groups are for weaklings.   23
You've got to get hold of yourself.   25
She is holding up so well.   27
Cheer up.   31
No sense crying over spilt milk.   33
This is nature's way.   35

"HURRY UP" CLICHES
You're not your old self.   38
Out of sight, out of mind.   40
Time will heal.   43
You're young, and you will be able   45
    to make a new life for yourself.
I just don't understand your behavior.   46
You should be over this by now.   49
Life goes on.   51
No sense dwelling on the past.   53

"GUILT" CLICHES
If you look around, you can always find   56
    someone who is worse off than yourself.
This is the work of the devil.   58
If I were you, I would do it this way.   61

Count your blessings. 63

Only the good die young. 65

If you had been a better Christian, 67
  this would not have happened to you.

Think of all your precious memories. 71

It's a blessing. 73

"GOD" CLICHES

God needs him more than you do. 76

He is happy now for he is with God. 78

God needed some new flowers for 81
  His garden in Heaven.

God did this to show us how powerful 83
  He is.

It was God's will. 85

God never gives us more than 89
  we can handle.

God helps those who help themselves. 91

"DISCOUNT" CLICHES

They know how I feel. 94

I know just how you feel. 97

Silence is golden. 98

If there is anything I can do, 100
  just call me.

You can have more children. 102

It's better to have loved and lost 104
  than never to have loved at all.

Be glad you don't have problems
  like mine. 107

Kids say the darndest things. 109

What you don't know, won't hurt you. 111

XIII

"BE STRONG" CLICHES

"Big boys don't cry."

Crying is therapeutic. The tears shed in sadness have a different chemical make-up from those shed in laughter or physical pain. It is nature's way of cleansing and healing. Men, as well as women and children, should be allowed to use this God-given way of relieving stress. More men die from stress-related diseases than women because of these suppressed feelings that have no other outlet. "Many Anglo-Saxon men beat the system of venting their grief by having heart attacks, one of the most prevalent results of losing a child," says Simon Stephens. (Stephens is the chaplain who founded The Compassionate Friends, an organization for bereaved parents and their families.)

In many other cultures, men are given permission to grieve and show emotion. However, in our death-denying American culture, we do not know how to deal with grief. We do not like to see men cry. From childhood on we teach men to be strong and in control of all situations, while we accept emotional, even hysterical, behavior in women in times of tragedy. We teach men to be stoic and unemotional and then we place them, ironically, in the two professions that probably require more feeling and compassion than any others - medicine and religious ministry. We expect these men to show feelings that they have been taught all their lives to suppress. Then we are disappointed when they do not live up to our expectations.

Instead . . .

Such statements as, "Don't be embarrassed to cry," or "Go ahead and cry, because you will be more of a man to me," will allow males to show their feelings of humanness in nature's most natural way. Men and boys need to be encouraged to express their feelings if they are to relate honestly to the world. A man once told me, "I slept like a baby the night my son died... I slept for an hour, then got up and cried, slept for an hour, then got up and cried, etc." St Augustine, the greatest poet of Christian antiquity, wrote after the death of his mother, "I didn't cry then, nor at the funeral, but later alone one night, I let the tears flow making a pillow for my heart."

"The children are flexible . . .
they will bounce back."

Yes, children are flexible, but even children can break. Grief in children does exist. It is not just an adult problem. Fortunately, we are slowly beginning to address the problem of how to help children grieve. Bereaved children feel anger, fear, isolation, guilt, loneliness, and loss with the same intensity as adults. They need to be given the means and opportunities to vent these overwhelming feelings. In fact, because children have not yet learned how to disguise feelings as a coping technique, they are actually experiencing a purer and more potent form of these painful emotions. This is why children retreat into a fantasy world and are only able to grieve intermittently. Play is a familiar retreat for children just as grieving adults bury themselves in the familiar security of their office and job.

So often we think we are shielding them from hurt, but in most cases, we are only increasing their anxiety when events are shrouded in secrecy. We should deal openly and honestly with children at whatever level they are able to comprehend. Children will only absorb what they are able to tolerate emotionally. Let the children be as involved as they want to be in the funeral service and related activities, but do not force them. (For so long, children have been conspicuously inconspicuous regarding bereavement and the grief process.) Later, provide ways for them to talk and express their grief. They, also, have a long process to work through. This can be made easier with guidance and support from adults.

Instead. . .

Say, "I bet you will miss your sister. Would you like to talk about her?" or "Would you like to talk about your father? He was my friend and I miss him, too." Statements like this can open the door to more feelings and sharing. "I bet you are angry because your brother died. I would be," could let the child know that feelings of this nature are normal and acceptable. Childhood is a precious commodity, but because it is so fragile it can be greatly upset by grief that is unresolved and unattended.

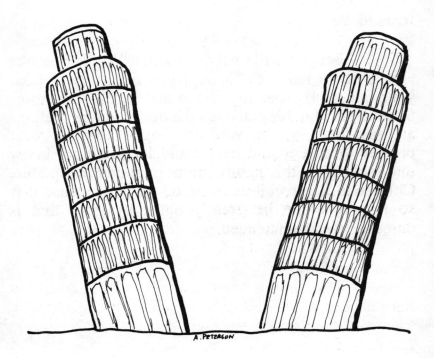

A. PETERSON

"You must be strong for your children."

You must also be strong for your spouse, your relatives, and your friends. This sounds great, but it seldom works. It is like telling a person who is having a heart attack to drop everything and help the person next to him who is also having a heart attack. I'm sure we all feel like we need to be strong, and may desperately want to be strong, but we cannot always be the Rock of Gibraltar for those we love. Sometimes we feel more like the Leaning Tower of Pisa. As one bereaved parent was told by her mother, "Your friends and relatives are coming to comfort you, but you will end up comforting them." Everyone feels so weak and helpless in this situation, and yet we all feel a need to provide the strength for those around us.

I am reminded of a lady I met on a plane several years ago. She was flying to Portland to visit her daughter. In the process of our conversation, she told me that she had another daughter who had died fifty years ago and the anniversary of her daughter's birthday was coming up in a few days. She expressed her anxiety about getting through that day without talking about it so she would not upset anybody during her visit. She was still being strong for her child fifty years later. Yet she cried in front of me - a total stranger. How sad it is that we are sometimes afraid to grieve in front of those we are the closest to because we are trying to live up to unrealistic expectations that have been placed on us either by ourselves or others.

Instead. . .

The above cliche suggests that we are to be like marble statues - rigid, cold, and unfeeling. Grief hurts, and feeling weak and frail is natural. Telling someone to be strong at this time denies them the right to a normal and natural grief response. You might say, "Why not share your feelings with your child? Perhaps you can lean on one another and help support each other?" Borrowing the philosophy from a country western song, "Let's fall to pieces together - why must be both fall apart?"

"Support groups are for weaklings."

Self-help groups are becoming a very necessary dimension of caregiving in our society today. People can reach out for needed support that normally was provided by close family units in years past. Unfortunately, the family unit has suffered due to an ever-increasingly transient society. Because self-help groups are relatively new in our culture, many people, through lack of understanding, see them as a means of prolonging grief and self-pity. People tend to have the misguided impression that being involved in a self-help group indicates that a person is weak and cannot cope properly, or that they are too poor to afford "proper counseling." The intentions of people who have adjusted and are trying to help others through the same experience are misunderstood as well. Self-help groups need people in all stages or the purpose of the group would be defeated. New members need to see successful role models; successful role models would not be necessary if there were no new members needing help. There is a great misconception in our society that Americans should handle their own problems and not burden others by asking for help. We all need to know that it is all right to ask for help. No one can deny the fact that self-help groups of all types are flourishing throughout the country because they do provide an atmosphere of positive growth and healing.

Anyone can grieve - just open up a vein. No one is immune to grief. It is a process we experience many times and for many reasons in our lifetime, and these reasons may have nothing to do with death. We may grieve over a lost job, loss of health, or loss of self-esteem, and ironically, grief is a subject with which we are least willing to deal. A friend of mine used to say, "No sense crying over something that can't cry over you." This certainly would limit us to only a few brief moments of sadness in our life.

Instead . . .

Physical illness goes hand in hand with emotional stress. Grief causes stress, and we have more stress-related illnesses in our society today than ever before. Much of this can be avoided by encouraging the bereaved to seek help, either professionally or through a support group, if they seem to be lost or stuck in their grief. Also, give them support and encouragement if they express the desire to seek help.

Likewise bereaved people have a responsibility to teach others how to help them. We would not let someone stand on our foot in a crowded elevator, and yet we let others stand on our feelings because we will not speak out. We need to let our needs be known, instead of begrudgingly accepting the painful things that are said and done.

"You've got to get hold of yourself."

It is natural for the people associated with a bereaved person to want that person to return to normal as soon as possible. But it is also a fact that it is uncomfortable to be around a grieving person, and so for selfish reasons of our own we want to speed up this process. It is almost as if we are afraid to give this person permission to grieve for fear that they will wallow in our sympathy and never want to get well. No one wants to get well more than the bereaved person, but we must let them give voice to their suffering before the process of healing can even begin. Those in mourning need to let the pressure escape slowly to avoid blowing off the lid. The Jewish "Shiva," the first seven days of intensive mourning, is a wonderful step in the right direction. At one time in America people wore a black arm band for a year to let others know they were in mourning. The wife of Jefferson Davis wore a "mourning pin" after her five-year-old son, Joseph, died in 1864. It was also customary in the 1800s to weave beads together with the hair of the deceased to form a wreath. This wreath was placed on the coffin, and after the funeral it was placed in a prominent place in the home, such as over the mantle. These symbols excused people from having to pretend they were not hurting.

One of the most unusual stories about grief was told to me by a young woman. When she was twelve her cousin died. They were like sisters, and her grief was overwhelming. She fashioned a small tombstone out of materials at hand, and set aside an area in her room which represented the grave of her cousin. In this way she could feel close to her and visit her whenever she wanted. (She had not been allowed to go to the funeral or the actual grave.) She would even put flowers on this make-believe grave. Had she been allowed to go to the gravesite this ritual probably would not have been necessary. As it was, she found a way of expressing her grief, and soon her "pretend grave" was no longer needed.

Instead . . .

To onlookers, some grief behavior seems very strange, but we must remember that all people are different and will handle grief in their own way. What works for one may not work for another. Support other's needs to cope with grief, and don't be judgmental about how they choose to do it.

"She is holding up so well."

As Joseph Bayly so appropriately stated in his book, The Last Thing We Talk About, "Many of us move into a house of mourning with our heavy artillery: we spend time, cook food, take care of children, do the wash...," but after the funeral, we disappear, sometimes never to be seen or heard from again. Sometimes a house of mourning takes on an almost carnival-like atmosphere with everyone eating, talking, and scurrying around. Bereaved people are in an emotional and physical state of shock and, in most cases, do not even remember most of the events of those first few days. Shock, "nature's hypo," takes effect immediately, but it may take weeks to wear off. Comforters may be misled by this initial response of a bereaved person into thinking that they are doing fine.

I remember being left alone in what seemed to be an operating room only minutes after being told that my son was dead. The nurse had left to go get me a "coke." I wanted to destroy that room, but I knew that if I "appeared to freak out," I would be heavily sedated and I didn't want that. (I was already becoming more and more sedated by my own body.) Later that evening, relatives who had brought food over insisted that we eat - it was dinner time and this was the "normal" thing to do. My son's father proceeded to throw his full plate of food against the nearest wall. It was my sentiment exactly. (It reminds me of the time he literally shoved two huge bowls of food and milk in the face of our cat who was in the process of giving birth to five kittens - as if she was going to chow down on a big meal at a time like that.)

I have faint memories of visiting with some guests, making sure that other guests were properly introduced - all the things a good hostess should do. After the funeral was over I do not remember one thing that happened for the next three weeks and, yet, I was functioning on what appeared to be a normal level of awareness.

We praise the bereaved person's zombie-like behavior by telling them how brave they are and how well they are holding up. Then the funeral is over, the people are gone, the food is all eaten, and the flowers are starting to wilt. This is when bereaved people realize the nightmare is for real. This is when they need your additional support. This is when they need a friend - those wonderful "neighbors of the heart." It is much easier to be in the first wave to hit the beach for there is support in numbers. It seems much harder to be with the bereaved "one on one" after the funeral has passed, but just remember that all they really need is for you to be there and be a good listener.

Instead. . .

It is vitally important to keep in touch after the funeral, long after the time that you think they are probably doing alright. Plan some quiet time with the bereaved when they can talk and you can listen. Statements like, "Let your feelings out," or "Don't feel that you have to be strong for me," will be helpful to the bereaved person. Avoid statements that encourage them to hide their feelings and, thus, deny their grief. A wonderful way to show your love and concern is to remember the anniversary of the person's death with a card or gift for the bereaved. It is so easy for the bereaved person to feel that everyone else has forgotten and they will have to face these difficult times all alone. Anniversaries and holidays will be difficult for years to come, but, so often, the support stops long before even the first year has passed.

"Cheer up."

This can be a problem when friends and relatives contradict the feelings of the bereaved person. "Cheer up," an annoyed husband will tell his wife, "life isn't all that bad." But to the bereaved person it is that bad or even worse. That's why well-intended distractions, such as a trip to the movies, often backfire. The bereaved person can't shake the mood of depression; consequently, the person who tried to help may become angry. The bereaved person may then begin to feel that no one understands and this leads to more hurt and anger. This is a common scenario which can cause many problems.

When the bereaved person does begin to smile, laugh. and enjoy life again, even if it is in small doses at first, there may be a sense of guilt that the memory of the loved one is being betrayed. So be careful not to hurry the bereaved person back to a state of happiness before he or she is ready. Too often grieving people are put in a position of feeling as if they have to apologize for their sadness. This may cause them to appear to be well, when actually, they have just become better actors, masking their grief with fake smiles. This charade may do nothing more than prolong the grief process or cause other complications. This occurs all the time in our society.

We learn at an early age to put up a good front for the viewing audience - our public. I witnessed a five-year-old child "in training" while in the Post Office one day. She was asked by a postal clerk, "How are you today?" When the little girl did not respond, the conversation between her and her father went something like this:

Father - "Aren't you going to answer the lady?"
Daughter - "What should I say?"
Father - "Tell her you are fine."
Daughter - "What if I'm not fine?"
Father - "Tell her you're fine anyway."

Instead . . .

Bereaved people must heal from the inside out, and most do if we give them time. By saying something like, "I know the loss of your loved one must make you terribly sad, and you have a right to be," we are not making unrealistic demands at a time when it may be impossible for them to meet our expectations. Sure we want them to "cheer up" and "be happy" because we love them; but maybe right now they just can't do it. Give them space and time to work out those feelings.

"No sense crying over spilt milk."

This is one of those cliches that hopefully no one says to a bereaved person, but may insinuate by their actions and words. I once knew a lady who was told by her dying mother that she did not want any tears shed after her death. Three years later this poor daughter was a nervous wreck trying to keep her mother's wish. She had fought back tears all these years, and when she would cry she felt guilty. By asking the bereaved to deny the process of grief we place a burden on them which is not only unrealistic but unhealthy.

We even carry this cliche so far as to hear people say that they don't want their loved ones to mourn at all when they die. People say things like, "Have a party. Break out the champagne and celebrate. No mourners for me." (Rock Hudson insisted that his friends throw a big party after his funeral, which they did, complete with champagne and caviar.)   A lot of "backwardology" exists in our society   regarding funerals. Someone once said, "Funerals are an amazing tradition - they throw a huge party for you on the one day they know you can't come."

By joking about death and making light of the tragic effects it has on people, we are actually trying to cover up the fear and anxiety we, as a society, have about our own mortality. Actually, it's logical to fear death because life matters. When we turn away from "the face of death" we deny ourselves fundamental insight into the relationship between living and dying.

How often do we hear jokes regarding terminal illness, tragic accidents, funerals, and the like? How often do we see the theme of death presented in a light and comical way in commercials and cartoons? To many, death is something that happens in the movies, not something that can actually touch us where we live and breathe.

Instead . . .

We cannot prevent our loved ones from hurting after we are dead just by telling them not to hurt. Nor can we make the fear of death go away by joking about it or trying to ignore the hurt it causes. By saying, "You will shed a lot of tears because this will hurt, and these tears will be good for you," you are encouraging them to cry and get in touch with their feelings. Only in this way can they begin to deal with them. It makes a lot of sense to cry over spilt milk; it may prevent a heart attack or nervous breakdown later on.

"This is nature's way."

There seems to be a great insensitivity toward parents who lose stillborns or premature babies. Not only do we discount the importance of the loss, but, in some cases, we neglect to even consider it a loss or cause for grief. We tend to equate the degree of love with time involved. Thus, it is easy to assume that grief will be minimal at best because they did not really know the child. Many people in this category hesitate to consider themselves bereaved parents because society puts so much pressure on them to get over this one in a hurry. These parents are left wondering if they have earned the right to grieve. If they do decide to grieve openly, they may or may not get a sympathetic response. Also, we should realize that there is a justifiable fear that maybe the same thing will happen again if they have another child; sadly enough, it sometimes does.

Instead. . .

Statements such as, "It must be so hard to lose a baby," or "I'm sure you had many hopes and dreams for the future," will show that you are really in touch with their pain. If we can imagine how hard it must be for these parents to leave the hospital empty-handed and go home to an empty nursery, then we can surely understand why these bereaved parents deserve all the compassion we can give them.

"HURRY UP" CLICHES

"You're not your old self."

Grief would not be as difficult if we could have some educational and psychological preparation. But trying to educate anyone about grief is very hard to do, because most people feel they will have no use for this information. There is the common belief that "that sort of thing always happens to the other guy; not to me."Plus, our feelings of immortality block out our desire to learn. Once grieving begins, it is equally hard to explain what is happening. It is like trying to teach swimming to a drowning person. To add to the difficulty, the grief process has a way of sweeping people off their feet as though they were caught in an undertow.

Thus, death-related grief nearly always has a jarring impact on a person's self-concept and relationship with others. A person's whole system of values and priorities can be temporarily turned upside-down. It is true that bereaved people are not their old selves. It is also true that, because of this profound experience, they will never be the same again.Alcoholics Anonymous has a wonderful way of describing this phenomenon. It's called the "pickle story." It goes like this... a cucumber can always become a pickle, but a pickle can never become a cucumber again. Once people have become bereaved and lost their sense of innocence and invincibility, they are changed forever.

With each new life experience, all of us are molded -
sometimes for the better and sometimes for the worse.
The bereaved person is not the same in our eyes, but
neither are we the same in the eyes of the bereaved.
When a tragedy occurs everyone affected by that
tragedy will change, some more than others. A
bereaved person is like a piece of burned toast - some
will make do with the burned toast as it is, some will
scrape and scrape until it looks and tastes like they
want it to, and some will simply discard the toast and
start over with a new piece of bread. Thus, some
relationships are strengthened, some renewed, and
unfortunately, some are dissolved.

Instead . . .

This cliche could be interpreted to mean that you
don't like the person the way they are now. Give the
bereaved time, and maybe you will see that out of this
painful process will arise a person who is even better
than the "old self." The "new self" may be stronger,
wiser, and more sensitive. With your love and support
a sense of wholeness can once again exist where grief
had threatened to tear not only individuals but
relationships apart.

"Out of sight, out of mind."

Presumably this is never verbalized, but based on this premise, so many well-meaning friends will encourage the bereaved to remove any reminder of the deceased such as pictures, articles of clothing, or other personal belongings. This can have disastrous effects, because the bereaved person is rarely ready for such a drastic step. I know of more than one case where "friends" came in and literally stripped a house of all the deceased's personal belongings while the funeral was in process. Some bereaved people want all reminders removed for a while until the pain eases, but many don't. At any rate, no one should make that decision for the person. Unfortunately, a conflict may arise within a family where some members may want reminders removed, and other members may want them left in place. If at all possible, the wishes of each member should be respected and some compromise reached. I once was told of a situation where the parents chose to handle their grief by removing every reminder of their dead son to the point of not even letting their daughter have a picture of her brother. This sister managed to keep one tiny school picture which she has secretly guarded for the past ten years for fear that her parents would find out. How sad.

Instead...

Let the person clean out the room of the deceased and dispose of personal belongings when it is comfortable for them to do so, for this is one of the most painful tasks they will ever have to perform. If pictures or other possessions of the deceased give comfort to the bereaved person, they should be kept and displayed if desired.

Whenever the opportunity presents itself, it is appropriate to refer to a picture or memento when in the bereaved person's home. Let them know that you, too, have not forgotten the deceased person. If you were close to the deceased and have such items, it is also a touching reminder for the bereaved person to see a picture or memento of the deceased in your own home.

"Time will heal."

Almost everyone can endure severe pain if they know that it will only last a given period of time. But newly bereaved people have a hard time believing that this terrible pain won't last forever. Therefore, it seems all the more unbearable. During this period of time, which may last for several years, the bereaved person is experiencing emotions such as anger, fear, guilt, despair, and loneliness. These emotions may ebb and flow in such a way as to defy time or reason. This grief processs has a negative connotation because of its association with death, loss, and suffering. I like Doug Manning's suggestion for a new way of looking at grief in his book <u>Don't Take My Grief Away From Me</u>. He says, "Grief is not an enemy - it is a friend. It is a process that is trying to get you back to a well state physically and emotionally. Flow with it - don't fight it."

In our Western culture, death is something to be tamed and dominated. In Eastern cultures, death flows naturally as a partner with life. This makes the grief process flow more naturally as well.

Instead . . .

By saying, "You must feel as if this pain will never end," you are showing that you understand how they are feeling right now. Try to concentrate on the present - not how they may feel three years from now. To the bereaved, each day can seem like an eternity.

Yes, time will heal - if we let it. But the process of grieving takes more than just time. It requires a desire on the part of the bereaved to want to actively work through the kaleidoscopic feelings that will result. So, be careful not to pass this cliche off as a quick and easy antidote for a difficult and complex problem.

"You're young, and you will be able to make a new life for yourself."

Before making this statement, one should stop and think that maybe a new life is the very last thing that person wants. All they really want right now is to have the life they had. In time, most bereaved people do make a new life for themselves whether they are young or old, but this is not an expectation that they want to have thrown at them right off the bat. Don't expect this person to suddenly direct all their energy toward the future when there is so much unfinished work at the present. Grieving consumes a tremendous amount of physical and emotional energy, and the future will not be rewarding unless the present is dealt with in a constructive and productive way. Give them time. They know that a new life will come, and a different life will exist in the future. But, for now, they need time to grieve for the old life - the life they will never have again.

Instead. . .

By saying, "I know you will miss your loved one and the life you had together; I will, too," you are showing that you have a greater understanding for the feelings of that person. The future can surely wait a little while longer.

"I just don't understand your behavior."

Because of our death-denying culture, we do not accept grief as a normal, natural, and necessary process. Therefore, it is something that makes us uncomfortable. We need to understand that what is normal grief behavior is not necessarily normal behavior. Grief can cause a "big time" attack of the crazies. Helen Hayes describes the feeling perfectly when telling about her adjustment to widowhood. She admitted candidly, "For two years I was crazy as can be and still be at large. It was total confusion. How did I come out of it? I don't know, because I didn't know I was in it when I was in it." Keep in mind that in the early stages, which could include the first year or more, the bereaved person is not altogether rational. There is a preoccupation with the tragedy that prevents clear thinking. (In fact, there should be a group called D.A.M.P. - "drivers against mourning people." Many a bereaved person has driven the car with his or her mind consumed in thought and totally oblivious to the road.) These powerful emotions, never before experienced, can have frightening effects. One may literally think he or she is going crazy until a sense of normalcy returns to their daily life. Thus, if our society were more informed about the grief process, judgments would not be so harsh at times.

The other side of the coin is that bereaved people have to deal with a lot of irrational, inappropriate behavior from those around them. It is appalling how insensitive people can be. In many instances, this behavior comes from those closest to the bereaved. There is an almost unconscious, self-imposed sentence that one has to put up with this hurtful behavior because these are relatives and friends. This may lead to silent and unresolved anger that can smolder for years.

Instead . . .

For bereaved people, needs can grow out of proportion; every hurt and discomfort is magnified. These people want compassion, love, and understanding. Try to avoid heaping more pain and chastisement on them when their ego has already taken a severe blow. Instead, encourage them by saying, "I know you are doing the best you can under these horrible circumstances." Don't expect more than the bereaved person can give. No one can live up to our expectations all the time; thus, the more we expect from people the more we will be disappointed.

"You should be over this by now."

This is an area where there are probably as many opinions as there are grieving people. Not too long ago, the consensus was that one to three weeks was sufficient. Then six months became acceptable. Now, it seems many are prone to agree that two years or more is not unreasonable. This does not mean that a person will grieve with the same intensity from the moment they learn of the death until an inner resolution is reached. Obviously, the intensity of grief will subside as time passes, with many periods of what appear to be remissions and relapses. This is very normal and does not mean that the grief process, as a whole, is not working. Everyone grieves according to one's own timetable, and only they know what that timetable is. Bereaved people sometimes get caught "between a rock and a hard place." If they grieve too much, they are weak; if they grieve too little, they are accused of not loving enough. Who is to say what the perfect time limit is?

Fortunately, we are becoming more compassionate and understanding as a society. Research is beginning to show that grief is, indeed, an acceptable and legitimate process. As our society learns more about this phenomenon, it is hopeful that a growing tolerance will also develop.

Death education needs a "new hemline." The present one is old-fashioned and out of style. We do not have to accept a standard procedure just because that is the way it has always been done in the past. When a daughter was asked why she cuts the ends off of her roast before putting it in the pan she said it was because her mother always did it that way. When the mother was asked the same question, she said it was because her mother did it that way. Finally, when the grandmother was asked why she cuts the ends off of her roast, her reply was, "That was the only way I could get it into the size pan I had." Individually and as a society we must find new ways to handle the oldest problem of all - death.

Instead . . .

Maybe by saying, "I know it will take a long time for you to feel better, and I will help you as much as I can," we are giving them time to move at their own pace. Then we will not have to urge people to race through a process that requires slow and deliberate progression. Death ends a life, but it does not end a relationship in the survivor's mind. This person must struggle on toward some type of resolution which may never come.

"Life goes on."

Several years ago I attended a July 4th picnic with some friends. We had just sat down on the ground and begun to eat. A country western band was playing and everyone was keyed up for the rodeo to follow. As we ate, I began to notice a mild commotion between the bandstand and me. I soon realized what was happening. Fifteen feet in front of me a man was dying of a seizure. The band continued to play as the paramedics arrived. The food line continued to serve as the paramedics worked feverishly. The people at the picnic continued to joke, laugh, and eat. The most important thing on many minds at that moment was whether or not to go back for seconds. And the band played on. After about twenty minutes of frantic effort this man died and was carried away. A large, green trash can was immediately rolled over to cover the spot where he had vomited several times while resuscitation attempts were made. The trash can stood, like a giant tombstone, marking the spot where only moments earlier a human being had died. Within minutes, people were passing by the trash can, throwing in their used paper plates and empty beer cans. Life, indeed, was "going on" with hardly anyone missing a beat.

Instead. . .

So often it seems as if there is a blinding determination to make sure that "life goes on" no matter what happens. It is as if we are all actors in the play of life and "the show must go on." But when a loved one dies bereaved people want the whole world to stop and take notice. Something tragic has happened. The truth is, to most of the world, a loved one's death will go unnoticed. The sun will continue to rise and set and people will go on about their lives. But the bereaved person now feels that they have been set apart from life in general. To deal specifically with the bereaved person's life, you could say, "Life has dealt you a terrible blow. I know it will be hard for you in the months to come to live with this pain." As a consoler, you need to give credence to the seriousness of their tragic loss. Trite statements like, "Life goes on," or "That's life," offer such casual, almost flippant, solutions to difficult and devastating problems.

"No sense dwelling on the past."

All bereaved people know in their hearts that they must somehow learn to live with this tragedy and get on with their lives, but it is so hard to do. Sad as it seems, there is a fear of moving on because precious memories fade in the process. As time passes, it becomes harder to remember the exact color of their hair and eyes, the sound of their voice, how tall they were, the way they laughed. They are forever frozen in time while our chronological clock keeps ticking. (This can be especially strange if the bereaved person was younger than the person who died and now they are older. By this trick of nature younger siblings can become the older sibling, and children can become older than their parents.) The bereaved person is trying to insulate these memories from time's grasp for as long as possible; they are not dwelling on the past for negative reasons.

Instead. . .

Rather than trying to discourage them from thinking about that phase of their lives, encourage them to share their wonderful memories with you. We all take strolls down memory lane. Why are we so hesitant to do this with the bereaved? Very few people choose to live in the past forever, but it's nice to go back and visit.

"GUILT" CLICHES

"If you look around, you can always find someone who is worse off than yourself."

Each person's grief is unique and should not be compared to any other for the sake of lessening the pain. This is not a contest to see who will win the "consolation bracket." When my son died I derived no comfort from knowing that there were parents who had lost two, three, or even ten children. Bereaved people are so consumed with their own grief and its tragic ramifications that they cannot imagine a worse situation. Grief has a way of isolating the bereaved and making them feel as if they were the only one going through this terrible suffering and soul-wrenching emotions.

So many cliches, this one included, are meant to direct the attention of the bereaved away from their pain. Why do we do this? Do we really think that by diverting their attention we can keep them from hurting? Why can't we let people grieve? We can no more stop their pain than we can pervent the wind from blowing by turning our back on it. We may only delay and thus prolong the process for them.

Instead...

This cliche implies that the bereaved should feel guilty and ashamed for feeling such pain. It would be much better to gently encourage them to face their sorrow and slowly sort through the maze of emotions that will surely follow. The bottom line is that it is their own pain they will have to live with, not someone else's.

"This is the work of the devil."

When people say this they probably mean that this tragedy is so awful that only the devil could have done such a thing. But this cliche, or any similar comment, should be avoided because the intention could be misconstrued. If so, the results could be very painful to the bereaved person. I have known several parents who have had this said to them after the death of their child, and in every case, they were hurt and offended. First, anything related to the devil usually has an evil connotation. Secondly, these parents assumed that this cliche was meant to insinuate that either they or their children lacked faith and were, therefore, instruments of the devil. As you can see, this would be a terrible thing for any God-fearing person to try to live with.

Instead. . .

So many of us must have an answer for every occurrence in life. Is it God or the Devil... Good or Bad... Black or White? Neat, orderly lives can be disrupted when shades of grey creep in, as they almost always do. Suddenly, the "cut and dried" answers we have don't fit the questions being asked. The truth is there are questions for which there are no answers. At least, not answers that our humble intelligence can comprehend. Likewise, there are incidents for which there is no one to blame. It would be much more honest and accurate to just say, "I don't know why something this awful happened to you."

"If I were you, I would do it this way."

In "Much Ado About Nothing," William Shakespeare wrote, "Every man can handle grief but he who has it." And if it is your grief you are dealing with you will be devastated beyond belief and deaf to the claims of well-wishers that "it will pass." As sure as there is cellulite, there will be people - standing in line - waiting to tell you how to grieve. But they are treading on treacherous ground when they attempt to tell a bereaved person this. Unsolicited advice almost always falls on deaf ears and can be a cause for future resentment. If you have "been there, too" you can offer gentle guidance, but avoid forcing your ideas on the bereaved person. The beautiful words of the French novelist, Albert Camus, express what the bereaved person probably feels:

Don't walk behind me, I may not lead
Don't walk in front of me, I may not follow
Just walk beside me, and be my friend.

Unfortunately, today's translation might well read:

Either lead, follow, or get out of my way.

Instead . . .

An honest statement like, "I can't tell you what to do because I am not you, and I have never had this happen to me," would be much more appreciated. Being an expert usually requires experience coupled with frequency. Because we never lose the same person more than once through death and because each loss has its own special pain, no one can possibly be an expert at handling death.

"Count your blessings."

This cliche, like many others, implies a veiled criticism. Just because bereaved people are grieving for something or someone they have lost does not mean they are not grateful for what they still have. Grief has a way of focusing on what has been lost, not what is still here. Hopefully, as people work through the grief process, they will begin to appreciate even more what they now have and focus less on what they have lost. If a man loses his leg, he may be very grateful for the parts of the body that he still has while grieving severely for what he lost. At first, grief will center around how he will cope with his loss. Later, he will learn to walk with a new leg or learn to accomplish the same goals with only one leg. At the same time he may rely heavily on his other limbs to compensate for the one that is gone. It is a fact that a blind person's other senses become so finely tuned that they operate far above their normal capacity. The blessings that a person has can give him a reason to want to regain his emotional well-being, but they cannot replace what is lost.

Instead. . .

Avoid this cliche, because it can make the bereaved feel guilty for grieving at a time when they probably have many other things to be thankful for. Didn't Christ grieve over one lost sheep that had strayed from his flock? Keep in mind that grieving is necessary and can be a productive process leading to wholeness. Give them this time to heal just as a body needs time to heal when it has broken or lost a part. We would not encourage someone with a broken leg to go jogging, because we know that it would not be good for their physical well-being. We need to be just as considerate of a person's emotional well-being.

"Only the good die young."

Is this really true? If so, then we should all pray for death at birth. We all know that many good children and adults die seemingly before their lives have really begun or when they were making such wonderful contributions to society. But we also must acknowledge that many good people live to a very ripe old age. What is the basis for this cliche? Is it because we think of the young as automatically being pure and innocent - almost as if they have a built-in safety valve against evil? If young people die, we might assume that they have not had time to be exposed to the dirty, seedy side of life. Thus, it would follow that no corruption has taken place. But many adults who have been "exposed" still continue to be virtuous. Is it because the good have earned their reward early in life and no longer have to struggle? This could be a possibility. Or is it because we have a tendency to glorify the deceased to the point of almost enshrining them at times? Attributes can become so glowing that memories of faults or shortcomings fade in comparison, or sometimes disappear altogether. When a child is involved this tendency toward glorification is especially true. If this cliche is true, then is it also correct to say, "Only the young are good."

I'm sure there are many good, mature people who would not appreciate this cliche. It should especially be avoided around children. If they think "the good die young" you may suddenly have a little monster on your hands. Monsters won't qualify for this so-called "honor." Or they could feel that they are not desirable in other's eyes because they weren't the "good one."

Instead . . .

If you want to say, "She was such a good person," or "He was such a good child," then you are praising the one who died without casting a negative light on those who are still alive. This allows room for the living of all ages to also be good and worthwhile.

"If you had been a better Christian, this would not have happened to you."

There is a cultural myth that if you pray and read the Bible, you will have no problems during your lifetime. It also follows that when you die, St. Peter will be waiting for you at the Pearly Gates with his arms outstretched. When asked if the names of all who died in faith were inscribed on a scroll exhibited in Heaven, Thomas Aquinas, one of the giants of Christian history, replied, "So far as I can see this is not the case, but probably there is no harm done if somebody says it is so." We should all have such tolerance with other's religious beliefs, instead of feeling a need to cram one's philosophy of religion down another's throat.

This cliche is meant more to defend God, not help the sufferer. In fact, it is often used as a weapon against the sufferer. We all know the story of Job in the Bible. No more faithful servant of God ever existed, and look at the tragedies he had to endure. I'm sure we all know a Job who can serve as an example to show that this cliche is not true.

Instead. . .

Avoid any cliche or statement that is judgmental. The last thing bereaved people need is to be kicked while they are down. It is amazing how many bereaved people have had this or similar statements said to them - usually by people who consider themselves to be very religious. These same people should become more familiar with the biblical verse, "Judge not, that ye be not judged." (Matt.7:1)

"Think of all your precious memories."

Most comforters mean this as a way of consoling the bereaved because memories are one of the things that keep them going. The bereaved carry the memories of their loved ones in the sanctuary of their souls for as long as they live. When I was a child and someone wanted to express that something would last for a long, long, time, they would say it would last until Niagara Falls. Well, as long as Niagara Falls, the bereaved will remember their loved ones and always feel at least some pain over the loss. There will be memories alright... dusted with the ashes of dreams.

I remember the night my six-year-old son, Michael, couldn't sleep. After numerous attempts, I finally suggested he try "counting sheep." After about ten minutes, he came back to me, and with a very serious look on his face, asked, "Is it all right if I count fire engines instead?" It has been over eleven years since his death, and I still laugh out loud when I think of that incident. Sometimes memories of my son make me laugh and cry at the same time. It's wonderful to have memories, but it's bittersweet when you know that that is all they are or will ever be.

Instead. . .

"I know that memories are a poor substitute for having this person with you, but I hope they will give you some comfort." By saying this you are not insinuating that the bereaved person should be satisfied with just memories or feel ungrateful if memories are not enough. Also, do not be afraid to initiate conversation where memories can be expressed and shared.

"It's a blessing."

This is usually said about a person who has suffered a long-term illness or was mentally incapacitated. If the person was hopelessly handicapped or in severe pain, the suffering is now over. By this cliche, the comforter is looking at the fact that only the present problem has been solved. However, the bereaved person's focus is on the entire picture. Why did their loved one ever have to suffer from this terminal illness or ever be in a situation of prolonged pain and suffering? There is this nagging question, "Why did this have to happen to my loved one?" This can release a backlog of unresolved grief that has been stored up throughout the person's illness. Thus, a bereaved person who may have thought that they worked through most of their grief during the long illness may suddenly find themselves swamped with additional grief. This could catch the bereaved person off guard. We must remember that no one can fully prepare for the death of a loved one. There will always be at least some after-shock and period of mourning.

Instead . . .

Be careful with this statement, because it does tend to deal with only one piece of a much larger puzzle. "I am sorry that this ever had to happen and that your loved one had to suffer so much," is a better way to approach this. Ironically, it is often the bereaved person you hear say, "It's a blessing," or "It's for the best." This is usually because they can sense your discomfort and are trying to comfort you even in the midst of their own anguish. Bereaved people do not like to see those around them suffer any more than you like to see the bereaved suffer.

"GOD" CLICHES

"God needs him more than you do."

Those who use this statement are trying to soften the blow by reassuring the bereaved person that the cause is justified - "God needed them." This statement expresses a need to have to defend God, which we should never do. Some do find comfort in this statement in the same way that parents who send their children off to war find comfort in knowing that their son or daughter met the call to duty for their country. The poster with the familiar words, "Uncle Sam needs you," has instilled pride in the hearts of many a fresh recruit ...and if there must be war, then there must be soldiers to fight. I personally feel that there is no greater way to die than for a noble cause such as defending one's country or in the act of saving another's life. But we tend to transform this into a situation where God needs more soldiers, more firemen, more missionaries, and so forth, with Him in Heaven.

Most deaths are not so noble. We all would like to give credibility and honor to the endless number of senseless deaths that occur because it is unbearable to think that anyone dies in vain. But how could we be so pompous as to believe that we have something that God doesn't have and needs so badly that He would take it away from us? Surely God does not meet His needs at such a cruel expense.

Instead. . .

This cliche tends to discount the needs of the bereaved and can cause guilty feelings because they are not able to forgo their needs for those of God. By saying, "We know you needed this person and feel a great sense of loss," we are focusing on the real issue. Maybe what we are really trying to say by this cliche is that there is a spiritual connection between God and the souls of mankind, and God is happiest when this connection is complete by man's soul returning to its Maker. The timing of deaths are not designed by a selfish God who ignores our needs.

"He is happy now for he is with God."

Unless you have the mountain-moving type of faith, this statement can cause a severe knee-jerk reaction such as, "Yes, but what about me?" A lady once told me that she found comfort in these words the first few times they were said to her after her son's death. But she said these same words began to enrage her after the fiftieth time she heard them. She wanted him here. How dare he be happy while she was so miserable? I am sure we would all agree that if the deceased person is with God, then he or she must be happy. But, for some, this is little consolation when it is all the bereaved can do just to wade through their own grief and loneliness. As time goes by, most bereaved people do find comfort in these words. But when the grief is so fresh, it is difficult for bereaved people to delight in their loved one's triumph into glory when all they can feel is unbearable pain and loss.

Because of a basic need to survive, people become selfishly engulfed in their own needs during grief. It is this self-centered behavior that keeps people from surrendering to total despair, and hopefully forces them to fight their way out of this black hole. This temporary selfishness can work in a positive way, and we should not try to divert the bereaved from this process.

Instead...

We could help bereaved people much more by focusing on the pain they are feeling than by telling them how wonderful the deceased must be feeling now. Try saying somthing like, "We know you are hurting terribly. We wish we could take the hurt away." Or, "You made his life so happy here on earth. You have much to be proud of." The bereaved person is feeling lousy enough without insinuating to them that their loved one was not satisfied with their life on earth.

"God needed some new flowers for His garden in Heaven."

This is a cliche that we hear expressed so often, and there are numerous poems with this theme. Some may find it consoling to have their loved one equated to a petunia, zinnia, or rosebud; most do not. It is a rather trite way to explain to adults who may be going through the worst tragedy of their lives that this is why that tragedy happened. Euphemisms should be avoided at all cost, both with adults and children, because they tend to skirt around the truth and avoid reality which must be faced sooner or later. Euphemisms often create anxieties and fears that are more harmful than the truth would have been. Two problems have now been created where once there was one. You have to "untell" the first lie, and, then, tell the truth. Now, even the "real truth" may not be as acceptable as it would have been the first time because your credibility is now jeopardized. Just as one should not tell a small child that their dead grandfather is "away on a trip" or that their dead parent is "just sleeping," so one should not tell an adult that their loved one is now a flower in God's garden.

Instead. . .

What you are really trying to say by this cliche is, "Your loved one is important to God and has a very special place awaiting them in Heaven." Why not say just that? This makes more sense than talking about flowers and planting gardens. Euphemisms are just another way of avoiding the reality of death.

"God did this to show us
how powerful He is."

"God did this to punish us for our sins." "God did this to teach us a lesson." I am sure that some find comfort in these words. I am also sure that most of this comfort, if not all, is felt by the giver of these words rather than by the receiver. We would not expect our worst enemy to treat us this way, and, yet, some think that by these words they will instill a feeling of reverence and awe for the power of God. For many, a serious loss causes a shakedown and re-examination of their religious beliefs, and a statement like this only serves to increase their anger toward God. After all, who wouldn't be angry with a God who plays cruel games with their lives - just to show His power or teach them a lesson?

We are so bent on trying to explain the will of God that often a backfire effect can occur. In trying to make a person feel good about God, it can actually make them feel worse or renounce God altogether. An example of this is expressed by Loretta Lynn. "When my daddy died," she said, "I wondered why he'd been taken, so I wrote a song called 'Momma, Why Did God Take My Daddy?' - which was exactly how I felt. Then when Mamma died, I again wondered why God had taken her because she wasn't all that old. But when my son died, I just felt there was no God."

Instead. . .

It would be much kinder to say, "God doesn't want these awful tragedies to occur any more than we do, and just as we are crying for the loss of our loved one, so also, is God shedding tears of sorrow." Or we could say, "God is a caring God, and He hurts when we hurt."

"It was God's will."

I'm sure that anyone who has ever gone through the process of grieving has had many times when the old "hippity-hop...ain't life great" attitude just wasn't there. I must admit that at times I have been a bit negative - not to mention angry, caustic, and downright bitter. For many people a lot of these feelings come from a confusion about what part God plays in events in their lives, especially tragic events. Many people cannot stand to think that things can happen haphazardly without rhyme or reason. Thus, we say, "If it were meant to be, it will be." In this way even random events appear to have a purpose. When tragic situations occur that have perfectly natural explanations we insist that God deliberately caused them. Plus, we are expected to accept this adversity with stoic obedience. Even Jesus showed emotions of anger and self-pity and felt deserted at different times in His life.

I would like to share with you a way of accepting "the will of God" that has given me great comfort. In a book appropriately titled, <u>The Will Of God</u>, by Leslie D. Weatherhead, God's will is divided into three types: God's intentional will, God's circumstantial will, and God's ultimate will. God's intentional will is seen as His original plan for the well-being of mankind. God's intention is that only good things should befall mankind such as good health, happiness, and peace of mind. But because of man's imperfect nature, and because God has created an orderly world where behaviors have predictable consequences and results have explainable causes, sometimes situations end in tragedy. If a body becomes infected with a disease either due to abuse, neglect, or simply a weak physical make-up, illness or possibly death could occur. This is a law of nature; not a deliberate act of God, but an orderly occurrence explainable through events of nature. Because the world is made the way it is, these events will happen occasionally. This is God's circumstantial will. If it were not in force we could play all sorts of games such as jumping from high buildings with the assurance that God would reach out his hand at the last minute to catch us.

Finally, there is God's ultimate will. Anyone would be foolish to presume to know God's master plan except to say that He has promised the ultimate redemption of mankind. God has the power to take the shortcomings and imperfections of man and mold them into ultimate good. This is why we so often see good and noble causes grow out of senseless, tragic events. The trouble arises because we use the general phrase "the will of God" to cover all three, without any distinction among them. So often we say, "It is

God's will," when actually it is man's imperfection at work. And sometimes things happen that are freak accidents and have no logical explanation. Why can't we leave them at that.

Instead . . .

The bereaved person would surely get more comfort if you were to say, "You are a good person, and this is a terrible and unfair tragedy to have to go through," or "Some things that happen are tragic and make no sense." Stop right there. Don't feel as if you have to explain by blaming God, the proverbial scapegoat.

"God never gives us more
than we can handle."

To believe and find comfort in this statement, we must assume two things; first, that God deals out these tragedies, and second, that all of us overcome and successfully cope with adversity. Since some people do have nervous breakdowns and some even commit suicide because of their inability to handle stress, it is hard to find validity in this cliche. It sounds good and it would be nice if it were true. But is it? Over 58,000 servicemen died in the war in Vietnam. It has been estimated that the number of veterans who have committed suicide since their return from Vietnam actually exceeds this number. Thus, from this one event, more than 58,000 men have chosen to take their own life because they could not bear to live with the horrors they had endured. On a more personal note, the year before my son died I was teaching school and had befriended a boy in my class named Tim. He had many problems at home and with his peers. I think I might have been the only friend he had. At a church service the night before my son's funeral Tim made a big point of coming up to me and telling me how sorry he was. I can still see him standing there. A few months later Tim was dead. He hanged himself in a jail cell. He was thirteen.

It is also unfair to assume that if people do not handle stress, then God is not active in their lives giving them the strength they need. We should not put a heavy burden of coping on the shoulders of bereaved people when their hurt seems insurmountable. I have always loved the comparison of a large task to that of "eating an elephant." At first the thought is overwhelming, but if we think of eating small pieces over a long period of time, it becomes much more feasible, although perhaps never palatable. One of the favorite slogans of Alcoholics Anonymous, probably the largest self-help group in the world, is "one day at a time." This slogan has been the salvation of millions.

Instead. . .

Be a little kinder and more compassionate by saying, "This must seem like more hurt than you can stand to bear all at once. Try to deal with it a little at a time until you get stronger." This way you will not make bereaved people feel like they must recover quickly to prove their faith.

"God helps those who help themselves."

But it would be more appropriate to say, "God helps those who stop hurting themselves." In his book, <u>When Bad Things Happen To Good People</u>, Rabbi Harold Kushner states,

> One of the worst things that happens to a person who has been hurt by life is that he tends to compound the damage by hurting himself a second time. Not only is he the victim of rejection, bereavement, injury, or bad luck; he often feels the need to see himself as a bad person who had this coming to him, and because of that drives away people who try to come close to him and help him. Too often, in our pain and confusion, we instinctively do the wrong thing. We don't feel we deserve to be helped, so we let guilt, anger, jealousy, and self-imposed loneliness make a bad situation even worse.

Bereaved people feel so "singled out" by fate that they even begin to think that they look physically different - like suddenly there is an ugly black mark on their forehead for all the world to see. Because society likes to preach that rewards follow good and punishment follows evil, it is easy for this "outer ugliness" to seep deep into the marrow of their bones. Almost all bereaved persons have to deal with negative feelings that are either self-imposed or imposed by others, whether justified or not. During the grief process people are almost constantly bargaining with their emotions in an attempt to eradicate these negative elements for they can surely destroy self-esteem and even life. If they persist, irrational thoughts and bad feelings can slow down or even halt the grief process. In <u>For Those Who Live</u>, Kathy LaTour suggests that, "Sometimes we can become so insulated by feelings that we are not only resistant to those trying to come in but also to those trying to get out."

Instead . . .

Our society discourages asking for help. We are supposed to be strong and solve our own problems, not burden others. In many, if not most, support groups it is safe to say they are lucky if they reach 10% of the people needing that particular type of support. The other 90% either cannot, will not, or have not asked for help for reasons that only they, themselves, can answer. Far too many bereaved people suffer silently and needlessly. Nowhere does it say, "God helps those who do it all by themselves." One could comfort best by saying, "You do not need to go through this alone. I know you are doing the best you can to get through this and I want to help you." Or you could say, "I know at this time it must be hard for you to believe that God is a loving God who will support you through this horrible tragedy."

"DISCOUNT" CLICHES

"They know how I feel."

Don't presume that grieving people know you care and are thinking about them. Tell them. At this time grieving people are supersensitive and may interpret your silence or avoidance as meaning that you don't care. Many feelings have been hurt needlessly because actions and words were misinterpreted. Because most of us feel uncomfortable around a bereaved person (this is only natural) and because our culture does not know how to deal with grief, fears of what to say and do lead to avoidance. This can be terribly harmful and hurtful for both the comforter and the comforted. The longer one stays away, the harder it will be to face that person. As a society we have even developed acceptable rationalizations for what may appear to be non-caring behavior. Statements such as; "Don't intrude," "Don't say the wrong thing," "Respect their privacy," excuse one from having to deal with these uncomfortable situations.

Instead. . .

You might try simply saying, "I am so shocked and hurt by what has happened to you that I am at a loss for words. I do not know how to tell you how awful I feel about your loss." Actually, the easiest and best thing to do is give that person a hug and just say "I'm sorry." It's almost too easy, but it works beautifully. Don't be afraid to leave some of your tears on the bereaved person's cheek if words are too painful. If a confrontation of any type is too difficult for you, then a sincere note of sorrow will let the bereaved person know that you care. The worst thing you can do is to do "nothing."

"I know just how you feel."

This statement probably causes more rage and anger in the bereaved than any other. No one knows how another person feels, because we are not that person, and we cannot know the depth of their feelings in any given circumstance any more than they can know ours. I sincerely believe that, in most cases, people who have suffered a tragedy tend to become more compassionate and sensitive, and are better able to empathize with another's adversity. Some, who have never been touched by tragedy, have an innate ability to experience this wonderful dimension of human nature that allows them to sense hurt and reach out to help. But no one can truly know how another feels. Sometimes we think we do, but we may not even be close.

Avoid playing the "apples and oranges game" by comparing the loss of a job, a pet, material possessions, or any other loss of this type with how the bereaved person must be feeling now.

Instead. . .

A more appropriate and honest statement would be, "I cannot begin to know how you feel because I have never had this happen to me. I just want you to know that I love you and hurt with you." Believe me when I say the bereaved person will appreciate your honesty.

"Silence is golden."

This proverb contains more than a grain of truth, but it can be misunderstood and, thus, misused. Silence can be golden if we sit quietly with the bereaved and let them draw strength and comfort from our desire to be with them, share their hurt, and let them talk about their loved one. Sometimes words just get in the way of our effort to console. But silence can become deafening in the months that follow the loss of a loved one if nobody will talk about the person that died. This "conspiracy of silence" is probably one of the cruelest side effects of grief. Most people think they are doing the bereaved person a favor by not talking about the deceased or even bringing up their name. Most bereaved people would love nothing more than for someone to talk about the deceased person with them. Many bereaved get the impression that maybe that person didn't really exist or that no one cares about the deceased person anymore. Sad as it may seem, close relatives are often the worst offenders. This is probably because their grief is so entwined with ours that it is almost as painful for them to deal with this terrible tragedy; therefore, it is equally hard for them to give us the support we need and expect.

How many times is the deceased member discussed at a family gathering? How often will we give a widow a chance to talk about her deceased husband? How often do we ask bereaved parents to tell us about their child? One of the greatest gifts you can give bereaved people is a friendly ear and the time to share the memories of their loved one with you.

Instead. . .

Statements like, "Tell me about your child," or "I sure miss your mother. We had so many fun times together," can open the door to a wonderful world of sharing and giving. People avoid mentioning the deceased because they don't want to upset the bereaved person by reminding them of anything painful. Ironically, it is more painful not to be given opportunities to talk about the deceased. Choose a time that is appropriate (not in the middle of a golf stroke) and appreciation will abound.

"If there is anything I can do, just call me."

This statement sounds nice. It sounds caring. In reality, however, it could be construed as a brush-off. Most bereaved people are so distraught for even months after the tragedy that the initiative to call should not be left up to them. After the death of my son, a very good friend of mine told me that she would not call and "bother me" and if I needed anything to call her. Apparently she had second thoughts because she began to call me every day. This procedure continued for about six weeks. We didn't talk long, but in those short conversations I could tell that she cared, that she was concerned, and that she was thinking about me. She helped me focus my attention on daily tasks that needed to be done when all I felt was confusion and disinterest. After eleven years, I am still deeply grateful for what my friend did.

Instead. . .

Try saying, "I will call you tomorrow (or in a few days), so if there is anything that you need, please let me know." Do not say you will call unless you absolutely intend to; if you say you will call, then by all means do so. Also, please do not be one of those people who lets the phone ring once and then hangs up, relieved by the fact that you did make your call as promised, but apparently no one was home. Keep trying. Brief calls from friends, as time goes by, mean much more than a one time hour's visit.

"You can have more children."

This can be a cruel and insensitive comment to make. In some cases, people cannot have more children. If this is the case, you are rubbing salt in an already open wound. Maybe the couple spent years just trying to have the child that is now dead. Perhaps they are now too old to have children or their health situation has changed. Even if they could have a dozen more children, that would not replace the child who died, as this statement suggests. When I first became involved with other bereaved parents, I met a family who told me of the loss of their son. Because their grief was so obviously devastating to all around them, I assumed that this must have been their only child. I was shocked to learn that they had ten other children. Never discount the importance of each child's life and the unique significance of that child to the family unit by suggesting that one child can replace another.

Instead. . .

We would not say to someone who has just lost their spouse, "You can get remarried," or to someone who has just lost a parent, "You can get another parent." In the same vein, we should not say to a bereaved parent,

"You can have more children." A more comforting statement would be, "I know you will miss this child and no one else will ever take their place," or, "I'm sure they will always have a special place in your heart."

"It's better to have loved and lost, than never to have loved at all."

Of all the cliches that bereaved people have tossed at them, this is probably one of the truest; it still does not wipe away the pain that person is going to have to suffer now and in the future. Magic wands are useless at a time like this. We are trying to coax the bereaved person into concentrating on the wonderful gift of love they shared with the deceased, while the bereaved person is consumed with the sorrow and loneliness they will now have to endure as a direct result of that love. This presents a contradiction of emotions. We are telling them to be thankful for having loved, but it is this very love that now causes them so much sorrow. And the more love there was, the more pain there will be. That's one equation that will never change.

Unfortunately, some go so far as to avoid love in the future as a protection from ever having to hurt this deeply again. This may be a conscious decision on the part of the one who has been hurt, or it may manifest itself in more subtle ways. No matter how hard we try to avoid love, most of us will love again because it is part of our basic nature.

Instead. . .

A more accurate statement to the bereaved would be, "I know your hurt seems unbearable, because you loved him so much." This doesn't take away the hurt, but to have that hurt acknowledged and accepted helps immensely.

"Be glad you don't have problems like mine."

It is amazing how oblivious some people are to the pain of others. The following story will show just what I mean. It is about a friend who had just lost her teenage son. She, in turn, had a friend who had recently lost her sight. The bereaved mother would take her blind friend to the grocery store, push her cart and at the same time pull her friend's cart. Her friend followed by holding onto the last cart. This strange caravan - one bereaved and one blind - was slowly making its way down one of the aisles when a mutual acquaintance approached them. Even knowing the circumstances of both, this person proceeded to tell them how lucky they were for not having to endure the latest flu bug, relating every detail pertaining to her bout with this nasty little critter. How having the flu can be as bad as losing a child or one's sight is a mystery, but comparisons of this nature are made all the time, and with little thought involved.

Instead. . .

Do not try to minimize the bereaved person's grief by trying to compare "war stories." If you have, indeed, suffered the same type of loss, then in most cases it is comforting to share. But do not do so if the intention is to make one loss sound more tragic than

another. To each person their grief is unique, and
their pain should be recognized and acknowledged as
such.

"Kids say the darndest things."

Children also suffer the pain of having hurtful and sometimes hateful things said to them by other children. Because kids are so uninhibited they may say things that an adult wouldn't dream of saying. I was shocked one day when I overheard a conversation between my five-year-old son, Chris, and a friend of his. We had recently moved to a new area, and Chris was explaining to another little boy that he had an older brother who had died. The boy responded, "You're lying. You don't have a brother. Show me where he is." (The kid must have been from Missouri - the "show me" state.) Obviously, my maternal instinct to protect my young from this "vicious attack" led me straight into the middle of their conversation and my son's defense. Believe it or not, this incident occurred at least one other time with my son and another child. My reaction the second time was not much different. Children not only say the darndest things, but what they say can be brutal. One young child who had lost a brother was asked by a friend, "Are the worms crawling on your brother?" I know this type of question would be both alarming and disarming to adults, but may roll off of a child's tongue with an innocence that is hard to believe.

On the other hand, some children have an uncanny way of knowing just the right thing to do. I am reminded of a story told to me by Art Linkletter, one of the greatest humanitarians of our time. "A little girl had just been next-door to console someone who had just lost a daughter and her mother said, 'Goodness, what did you say?' And the little girl said, 'Oh, I didn't say anything, Mommy; I just crawled up in her lap and cried with her.'"

Instead . . .

The sad thing is that we don't know what is being said or done to bereaved children by their peers. Children fumble through this awkward situation of bereavement as do adults. They say things they don't mean, and feel things they can't express. They are novices relying on the examples of adults who are uncomfortable with death and unfamiliar with grief. By teaching children about death, we are teaching them to value life. But we as adults must learn before we can be good teachers.

"What you don't know, won't hurt you."

There is an innate force that drives man to want to know all there is to know about himself. It is not unrealistic, selfish, or unreasonable to take the necessary steps to find answers to these important questions about one's heritage. In the case of adoption, adopted children have a right, and sometimes a need, to know about themselves: their medical history, who their parents were and what they were like, if there are brothers or sisters, and their nationality. In the common game of "heritage roulette," facts of this nature may be withheld or distorted causing harmful results. Many adopted children suffer from "misplaced nationality syndrome" - an illness that is not debilitating but certainly unsettling. While being raised by an Irish Catholic family, I was told all along that I was really Scandinavian. Forty years later, after finding my birth parents, I realized I was "really" German and Bohemian. God love my adopted parents for they were only trying to help me and told me what they believed to be true.

One may go through years or even a lifetime of mental gymnastics to reach a state of mind that is emotionally acceptable. This new state may be highly concocted but believable to the person who has to live with it. Children may use these gymnastics to rationalize why their parents gave them up. Birth parents may use this process to rationalize why they gave up their child. Many people decide to find out the truth. Each year thousands of adopted children and birth parents begin their search. It's one way of confronting a subtle but very real type of grief process. An important human bond has been severed, and grief will almost always result.

This can be very threatening to families of adoption, but we must remember that human love is flexible and expandable. Children can love and long for birth parents without taking away from the family they love and have come to know as their own. Birth parents can experience a true physical and emotional loss for a child they have never known while still loving other children they may have.

Instead. . .

Give support. Don't judge. It's easy to say, "Let sleeping dogs lie." But maybe you are not in a position to hear the barking - sometimes howling - that these "sleeping dogs" can cause. No one begins to look for their birth parents or child without a tremendous amount of soul-searching. It is a methodical, painful process that one does not take lightly, and once begun, one is not easily deterred.

Our society has grown too big too fast. We have learned to perform, produce, progress, and prosper with very little concern for the emotional expense involved. We have not cared enough for each other as fellow human beings. Why has it taken us so long to learn that we need each other? Grief causes a molestation of feelings that can only be soothed by the love and care of others. Everyone grieves for different reasons during their lifetime, and most grieve the old-fashioned way... they earn it.

BIBLIOGRAPHY

Claypool, John. Tracks of a Fellow Struggler. Waco: Word Books, 1974.

Grollman, Earl. Explaining Death to Children. Boston: Beacon Press, 1967.

Grollman, Earl. Talking About Death: A Dialogue Between Parent and Child. Boston: Beacon Press, 1970.

Grollman, Earl. What Helped Me When My Loved One Died. Boston: Beacon Press, 1981.

Keller, John E. Let Go, Let God. Minneapolis: Augsburg Publishing House, 1985.

Kushner, Harold S.. When Bad Things Happen to Good People. New York: Schocken Books, 1981.

LaTour, Kathy. For Those Who Live. P.O. Box 141182; Dallas, Texas 75214; 1983.

LeShan, Eda. Learning to Say Goodby. New York: MacMillan Publishing Company, Inc., 1976.

Linn, Erin, <u>Children Are Not Paper Dolls</u> . . . a visit with bereaved siblings. The Publisher's Mark; P.O. Box 6939; Incline Village, Nevada 89450; 1982.

Linn, Erin. <u>150 Facts About Grieving Children</u>. The Publisher's Mark; P.O. Box 6939; Incline Village, Nevada 89450; 1990.

Sarnoff-Schiff, Harriett. <u>The Bereaved Parent</u>. New York: Penguin Books, 1977.

Sharkey, Frances, M.D. <u>A Parting Gift</u>. New York: St. Martin's Press, 1982.

Weatherhead, Leslie D. <u>The Will Of God</u>. Nashville: Abingdon Press, 1976.

Westberg, Granger E. <u>Good Grief</u>. Philadelphia: Fortress Press, 1962.

NATIONAL SUPPORT ORGANIZATIONS

ADOPTION
- National Adoption Exchange
  1218 Chestnut Street
  Philadelphia, PA 19107
- Truth Seekers in Adoption
  P.O. Box 366
  Prospect Heights, IL 60070-0366
- Origins
  P.O. Box 105
  Oakhurst, NJ 07755
- Concerned United Birthparents
  595 Central Avenue
  Dover, NH 03820
- Right to Know
  P.O. Box 1409
  Grand Prairie, TX 75050
- Adoptees-in-Search, Inc.
  P.O. Box 41016
  Bethesda, MD 20014
- Yesterday's Children
  5945 Fiddletown Pl.
  Evanston, IL 60204

AGED
- Aging in America
  1500 Pelham Pkwy., S.
  Bronx, NY 10461
- Golden Ring Council of Senior Citizens Clubs
  3975 Sedgwick
  Bronx, NY 10463
- Jewish Association for Services for the Aged
  40 W. 68th St.
  New York, NY 10023
- National Support Center for Families of the Aging
  P.O. Box 245
  Swarthmore, PA 19081

119

ALCOHOLISM
- Alcoholics Anonymous World Services
  P.O. Box 459
  Grand Central Station
  New York, NY 10163
- Al-Anon Family Group Headquarters
  One Park Ave.
  New York, NY 10016
- Alateen
  One Park Ave.
  New York, NY 10016
- Adult Children of Alcoholics
  P.O. Box 421691
  San Francisco, CA 94142
- Children of Alcoholics Foundation
  540 Madison Ave., 23rd Fl.
  New York, NY 10022
- Mothers Against Drunk Drivers (MADD)
  669 Airport Freeway, Suite 310
  Hurst, TX 76053
- Students Against Driving Drunk (SADD)
  P.O. Box 800
  Marlborough, MA 01752
- National Association of Recovered Alcoholics
  P.O. Box 95
  Staten Island, NY 10305

CANCER
- Make Today Count
  P.O. Box 222
  Osage Beach, MO 65065
- Candlelighters
  2025 Eye St., N.W., Suite 1011
  Washington, D.C. 20006
- CanSurmount
  American Cancer Society
  90 Park Avenue
  New York, NY 10016

CANCER
- The Ronald McDonald House
  Golin-Harris Communication
  500 N. Michigan Ave.
  Chicago, IL 60611
- Institute for Attitudinal Healing
  21 Main St.
  Tiburon, CA 94920

CHILD ABUSE AND MOLESTATION
- National Center for the Prevention and
  Treatment of Child Abuse and Neglect
  1205 Oneida St.
  Denver, CO 80220
- Parents Anonymous
  22330 Hawthorne Blvd., Suite 208
  Torrance, CA 90505
- Parents United
  P.O. Box 952
  San Jose, CA 95108

DIVORCE
- Divorce Anonymous
  P.O. Box 5313
  Chicago, IL 60680
- Parents Without Partners
  7910 Woodmont Ave., Suite 1000
  Bethesda, MD 20814
- Single Dad's Hotline
  P.O. Box 4842
  Scottsdale, AZ 85258
- Mothers Without Custody
  P.O. Box 602
  Greenbelt, MD 20770

DRUG ABUSE
- Families Anonymous
  P.O. Box 528
  Van Nuys, CA 91408
- American Council for Drug Education
  6193 Executive Blvd.
  Rockville, MD 20852
- Straight, Inc.
  P.O. Box 21686
  St. Petersburg, FL 33742
- Toughlove
  P.O. Box 1069
  Doylestown, PA 18901
- National Federation of Parents for Drug-free Youth
  1820 Franwall Ave., Suite 16
  Silver Spring, MD 20902
- Do It Now Foundation
  P.O. Box 5115
  Phoenix, AZ 85010

HANDICAPPED
- National Amputation Foundation
  12-45 150th St.
  Whitestone, NY 11357
- National Association of the Physically Handicapped
  76 Elm Street
  London, OH 43140
- Just One Break
  373 Park Ave., S.
  New York, NY 10016
- Special Olympics
  1350 New York Ave., N.W., Suite 500
  Washington, D.C. 20005

HELP FOR THE DYING
- National Hospice Organization
  1901 N. Fort Myer Dr., Suite 402
  Arlington, VA 22209
- Children's Hospice International
  501 Slaters Lane, Suite 207
  Alexandria, VA 22314
- Concern for Dying
  250 W. 57th St.
  New York, NY 10107
- Society for the Right to Die
  250 W. 57th St.
  New York, NY 10107

LOSS OF A CHILD
- The Compassionate Friends
  P.O. Box 3696
  Oak Brook, IL 60522-3696
- SHARE
  St. John's Hospital
  800 E. Carpenter St.
  Springfield, IL 62769
- National Sudden Infant Death Syndrome Foundation
  2 Metro Plaza, Suite 205
  8240 Professional Place
  Landover, MD 20785
- Parents of Murdered Children
  1739 Bella Vista
  Cincinnati, OH 45237
- Resolve, Inc.
  P.O. Box 474
  Belmont, MA 02178
- Center for Sibling Loss
  The Southern School
  1456 W. Montrose
  Chicago, IL 60613

MISSING CHILDREN
- Child Find, Inc.
  1-800-431-5005
  1-800-IAM-LOST
- People Finders
  P.O. Box 651
  Batavia, IL 60510

RAPE AND BATTERED WOMEN
- National Coalition Against Domestic Violence
  1500 Massachusetts Ave., N.W., #35
  Washington, D.C. 20005
- House of Ruth
  459 Massachusetts Ave., N.W.
  Washington, D.C. 20001
- National Coalition Against Sexual Assault
  P.O. Box 7156
  Austin, TX 78713
- Batterers Anonymous
  1295 N.E. St.
  San Bernardino, CA 92405

SUICIDE
- Parents of Suicides
  15 E. Brinkerhoff Ave., 2nd Fl.
  Palisades Park, NY 07650
- National Save-A-Life League
  4520 Fourth Ave., Suite MH3
  New York, NY 11220
- National Committee on Youth Suicide Prevention
  230 Park Ave.,Suite 835
  New York, NY 10169

VETERANS
- Disabled American Veterans
  3725 Alexandria Pike
  Cold Spring, KY 41076
- Veterans of Foreign Wars of the U.S. A.
  Broadway at 34th St.
  Kansas City, MO 64111
- American Gold Star Mothers
  2128 Leroy Place, N.W.
  Washington, D.C. 20008
- Gold Star Wives of America
  600 Bethell St.,N.E.
  Leeds, AL 35094
- American Ex-Prisoners of War
  3201 E. Pioneer Pkwy #40
  Arlington, TX 76010

WIDOWS AND WIDOWERS
- National Association for Widowed People
  P.O. Box 3564
  Springfield, IL 62708
- Widowed Persons Service
  1909 K. St., N.W.
  Washington, D.C. 20049
- Theos Foundation
  410 Penn Hill Mall
  Pittsburg, PA 15235
- Widow and Widower Counseling and Referral Service
  Smylie Time Building
  8001 Roosevelt Bldg.
  Philadelphia, PA 19152